too many
TOMATOES
ZUCCHINI
PEPPERS

Publications International, Ltd.

Favorite Brand Name Recipes at www.fbnr.com

Pictured on the front cover *(left to right):* Mediterranean Vegetable Bake *(page 52)* and Southwestern Stuffed Peppers *(page 22).*

Pictured on the back cover: Pork & Peppers Mexican-Style *(page 18).*

ISBN-13: 978-1-4127-2440-1
ISBN-10: 1-4127-2440-6

Manufactured in China.

8 7 6 5 4 3 2 1

Microwave Cooking: Microwave ovens vary in wattage. Use the cooking times as guidelines and check for doneness before adding more time.

Preparation/Cooking Times: Preparation times are based on the approximate amount of time required to assemble the recipe before cooking, baking, chilling or serving. These times include preparation steps such as measuring, chopping and mixing. The fact that some preparations and cooking can be done simultaneously is taken into account. Preparation of optional ingredients and serving suggestions is not included.

TABLE OF CONTENTS

GREAT BEGINNINGS

Italian-Topped Garlic Bread

1 pound BOB EVANS® Italian Roll Sausage
1 (1-pound) loaf crusty Italian bread
½ cup butter, melted
2 teaspoons minced garlic
2 cups (8 ounces) shredded mozzarella cheese
2 cups diced tomatoes
8 ounces fresh mushrooms, sliced
3 tablespoons grated Parmesan cheese

Preheat oven to 325°F. Crumble and cook sausage in medium skillet until browned. Drain off any drippings. Cut bread into 1-inch slices. Combine butter and garlic in small bowl; brush bread slices with mixture. Arrange on ungreased baking sheet. Combine mozzarella cheese, tomatoes, mushrooms, Parmesan cheese and sausage; spread on bread slices. Bake 10 to 12 minutes or until cheese is melted and golden brown. Serve warm. Refrigerate leftovers.

Makes about 10 appetizer servings

Veggie Quesadilla Appetizers

10 (8-inch) flour tortillas
1 cup finely chopped broccoli
1 cup thinly sliced small mushrooms
¾ cup shredded carrots
¼ cup chopped green onions
1¼ cups (5 ounces) shredded reduced-fat sharp Cheddar cheese
2 cups Zesty Pico de Gallo (recipe follows)

1. Brush both sides of tortillas lightly with water. Heat small nonstick skillet over medium heat until hot. Heat tortillas, one at a time, 30 seconds on each side. Divide vegetables among 5 tortillas; sprinkle evenly with cheese. Top with remaining 5 tortillas.

2. Cook quesadillas, one at a time, in large nonstick skillet or on griddle over medium heat 2 minutes on each side or until surface is crisp and cheese is melted.

3. Cut each quesadilla into 4 wedges. Serve with Zesty Pico de Gallo.
Makes 20 servings

Zesty Pico de Gallo

2 cups chopped seeded tomatoes
1 cup chopped green onions
1 can (8 ounces) tomato sauce
½ cup minced fresh cilantro
1 to 2 tablespoons minced jalapeño peppers*
1 tablespoon fresh lime juice

Jalapeño peppers can sting and irritate the skin. Wear rubber gloves when handling peppers and do not touch your eyes. Wash your hands after handling peppers.

Combine all ingredients in medium bowl. Cover and refrigerate at least 1 hour.
Makes about 4 cups

7-Layer Ranch Dip

1 envelope LIPTON® RECIPE SECRETS® Ranch Soup Mix
1 container (16 ounces) sour cream
1 cup shredded lettuce
1 medium tomato, chopped (about 1 cup)
1 can (2¼ ounces) sliced pitted ripe olives, drained
¼ cup chopped red onion
1 can (4½ ounces) chopped green chilies, drained
1 cup shredded Cheddar cheese (about 4 ounces)

1. In 2-quart shallow dish, combine soup mix and sour cream.

2. Evenly layer remaining ingredients, ending with cheese. Chill, if desired. Serve with tortilla chips.   *Makes 7 cups dip*

Prep Time: 15 minutes

Tomato and Cheddar Tart

1 packaged unbaked refrigerated crust for 9-inch pie
2 tablespoons Dijon mustard
2 cups grated CABOT® Extra Sharp Cheddar (about 8 ounces)
1 pound vine-ripened tomatoes (3 to 4 medium), thinly sliced
1½ tablespoons extra-virgin olive oil
1 tablespoon chopped fresh thyme or marjoram

1. Preheat oven to 375°F.

2. On lightly floured surface, roll crust out into larger 13-inch circle. Transfer to large ungreased baking sheet, patching any holes.

3. With back of spoon, spread mustard evenly over crust, leaving about 1½ inches of edge uncovered. Distribute cheese evenly over mustard. Arrange tomato slices over cheese in overlapping rings. Drizzle evenly with olive oil.

4. Fold edge of crust over tomatoes, making small pleats with excess.

5. Bake tart for 30 minutes. Sprinkle tomatoes with thyme or marjoram and return to oven for 10 to 15 more minutes, or until tomatoes are crinkled on the edges and only slightly juicy. Cut into wedges and serve warm or at room temperature.

Makes 8 appetizer or 4 light entrée servings

Herbed Croutons with Savory Bruschetta

½ cup regular or reduced fat mayonnaise
¼ cup *French's*® Honey Dijon Mustard
1 tablespoon finely chopped green onion
1 clove garlic, minced
¾ teaspoon dried oregano leaves
1 long thin loaf (18 inches) French bread, cut crosswise into
 ½-inch-thick slices
Savory Bruschetta (recipe follows)

Combine mayonnaise, mustard, onion, garlic and oregano in small bowl; mix well. Spread herbed mixture on one side of each slice of bread.

Place bread, spread sides up, on grid. Grill over medium-low coals 1 minute or until lightly toasted. Spoon Savory Bruschetta onto herbed croutons. Serve warm.   *Makes 6 appetizer servings*

Note: Leftover croutons may be served with dips or cut up and served in salads.

Prep Time: 10 minutes
Cook Time: 1 minute

Savory Bruschetta

1 pound ripe plum tomatoes, cored, seeded and chopped
1 cup finely chopped fennel bulb or celery
¼ cup chopped fresh basil leaves
3 tablespoons *French's*® Honey Dijon Mustard
3 tablespoons olive oil
3 tablespoons balsamic vinegar
2 cloves garlic, minced
½ teaspoon salt

Combine ingredients in medium bowl; toss well to coat evenly.
                                        Makes 3 cups

Prep Time: 15 minutes

Creamy Salsa Dip

1½ cups prepared HIDDEN VALLEY® The Original Ranch® Dressing
2 tomatoes, peeled, seeded and chopped
½ cup shredded Monterey Jack cheese
¼ cup sliced almonds
¼ cup seeded and minced mild or hot green chile peppers
1 green onion, finely chopped
Additional sliced almonds for garnish
Fresh cilantro for garnish

In medium bowl, combine all ingredients, except almonds and cilantro for garnish; mix well. Refrigerate at least 1 hour before serving. Garnish with additional almonds and cilantro. Serve with taco chips or fresh vegetables. *Makes about 2 cups*

Tip: To seed a tomato, first cut it in half crosswise. Holding the tomato half, cut side down, over a bowl, gently squeeze the tomato to remove the seeds. If you prefer, you may carefully scoop out the seeds with a small spoon.

BelGioioso® Fontina Melt

1 loaf Italian or French bread
2 fresh tomatoes, cubed
Basil leaves, julienned
BELGIOIOSO® Fontina Cheese, sliced

Cut bread lengthwise into halves. Top each half with tomatoes and sprinkle with basil. Top with BelGioioso Fontina Cheese. Place in oven at 350°F for 10 to 12 minutes or until cheese is golden brown.
Makes 6 to 8 servings

Mini-Marinated Beef Skewers

1 boneless beef top sirloin steak (about 1 pound)
2 tablespoons dry sherry
2 tablespoons soy sauce
1 tablespoon dark sesame oil
2 cloves garlic, minced
18 cherry tomatoes
   Lettuce leaves (optional)

1. Cut beef crosswise into ⅛-inch slices. Place in large resealable food storage bag. Combine sherry, soy sauce, sesame oil and garlic in cup; pour over steak. Seal bag; turn to coat. Marinate in refrigerator at least 30 minutes or up to 2 hours.

2. Meanwhile, soak 18 (6-inch) wooden skewers 20 minutes in water to cover.

3. Drain steak; discard marinade. Weave beef accordion-fashion onto skewers. Place on rack of broiler pan.

4. Broil 4 to 5 inches from heat 4 minutes. Turn skewers over; broil 2 to 4 minutes or until beef is barely pink in center.

5. Garnish each skewer with one cherry tomato; place on lettuce-lined platter. Serve warm or at room temperature. *Makes 18 appetizers*

Alouette® 7-Layer "Fiesta" Dip

1 cup chopped tomatoes
1 cup chopped bell peppers
1 cup canned corn, drained
1 cup sliced scallions
1 (6.5-ounce) package ALOUETTE® Cilantro Lime or Garlic & Herbs
   Spreadable Cheese
1 cup shredded lettuce
½ cup sliced black olives

In a 1-quart clear glass bowl, layer ingredients in order beginning with tomatoes and ending with olives. Cover and chill for 1 hour for flavors to blend.

Serve with your favorite tortilla chips.   *Makes 6 servings*

Chili Dip

1 container (16 ounces) sour cream
1 medium tomato, chopped (about 1 cup)
1 can (4 ounces) chopped green chilies, drained
1 package KNORR® Recipe Classics™ Leek recipe mix
3 to 4 teaspoons chili powder

• In medium bowl, combine all ingredients; chill at least 2 hours.

• Stir before serving. Serve with corn chips or cut-up vegetables.
                                        Makes about 3 cups dip

Cheese Chili Dip: Stir in 1 cup shredded Monterey Jack cheese (about 4 ounces).

Tip: Use this dip to make Tortilla Roll-Ups. Simply spread Chili Dip on flour tortillas, top with cut-up cooked chicken, roll up and serve.

Prep Time: 5 minutes
Chill Time: 2 hours

FABULOUS MAIN DISHES

Pork & Peppers Mexican-Style

2 tablespoons olive oil
½ cup chopped green onions
¾ pound lean pork, cut into ¼-inch pieces
1 *each* red, yellow and green bell peppers, diced (about 2 cups)
1 teaspoon minced garlic
   Salt and black pepper
1 cup sliced fresh mushrooms
1 teaspoon cumin
1 teaspoon chili powder
½ teaspoon ground dried chipotle pepper (optional)
¼ cup (1 ounce) shredded Cheddar cheese
¼ cup sour cream

1. Heat oil in large skillet over medium-high heat. Add green onions; cook and stir 2 minutes. Add pork; cook and stir 5 minutes or until browned. Add bell peppers and garlic. Cook and stir 5 minutes or until bell peppers begin to soften.

2. Season mixture in skillet with salt and black pepper. Add mushrooms, cumin, chili powder and chipotle pepper, if desired. Cook and stir 10 to 15 minutes or until pork is cooked through and vegetables are tender.

3. Top each serving with cheese and sour cream.   *Makes 4 servings*

Chicken Provençal

1 tablespoon olive oil
2 pounds skinless chicken thighs
½ cup sliced green bell pepper
½ cup sliced onion
2 cloves garlic, minced
1 pound eggplant, peeled and cut into ¼-inch-thick slices
2 medium tomatoes, cut into ¼-inch-thick slices
¼ cup chopped fresh parsley *or* **2 teaspoons dried parsley**
¼ cup chopped fresh basil *or* **2 teaspoons dried basil**
1 teaspoon salt
1 cup fat-free reduced-sodium chicken broth
½ cup dry white wine

1. Heat oil in large skillet over medium-high heat. Add chicken; cook 2 to 3 minutes on each side or until browned. Remove chicken from skillet.

2. Add bell pepper, onion and garlic to same skillet; cook and stir 3 to 4 minutes or until onion is tender.

3. Return chicken to skillet. Arrange eggplant and tomato slices over chicken. Sprinkle with parsley, basil and salt. Add chicken broth and wine; bring to a boil. Reduce heat; cover and simmer 45 to 50 minutes or until juices from chicken run clear. *Makes 6 servings*

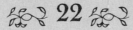
Southwestern Stuffed Peppers

   4 green bell peppers
   1 can (15 ounces) black beans, rinsed and drained
   1 cup (4 ounces) shredded pepper-Jack cheese
¾ cup medium salsa
½ cup fresh or frozen corn kernels
½ cup chopped green onions
⅓ cup uncooked long grain converted rice
   1 teaspoon chili powder
½ teaspoon ground cumin
   Sour cream

Slow Cooker Directions

1. Cut thin slice off top of each bell pepper. Carefully remove seeds, leaving pepper whole.

2. Combine beans, cheese, salsa, corn, onions, rice, chili powder and cumin in medium bowl. Spoon filling evenly into each pepper. Place peppers in slow cooker.

3. Cover; cook on LOW 4 to 6 hours. Serve with sour cream.

Makes 4 servings

Prep Time: 15 minutes
Cook Time: 4 to 6 hours

Bays® Welsh Rarebit

4 BAYS® English Muffins, split
2 packages (10 ounces each) frozen Welsh rarebit (Cheddar cheese
  sauce)
2 teaspoons prepared honey mustard
8 slices ripe tomato
8 slices bacon, preferably applewood smoked, halved crosswise,
  cooked crisp
3 tablespoons chopped chives

Lightly toast muffin halves; place split sides up on four serving plates.
Prepare rarebit according to package directions; stir in mustard. Top
muffin halves with sliced tomatoes. Arrange bacon over tomatoes in a
crisscross fashion. Spoon rarebit evenly over muffin halves and sprinkle
with chives. *Makes 4 servings*

Variation: For a heartier rarebit, place sliced deli smoked turkey breast
on muffin halves before topping with tomatoes, bacon, rarebit and
chives.

Shredded Pork Tacos

3 cups shredded or finely chopped cooked roast pork
1 cup chopped onion
1 clove garlic, minced
1 to 3 tablespoons diced jalapeño pepper
12 small flour tortillas, warmed
3 cups shredded lettuce
2 cups diced tomatoes
¾ cup (3 ounces) shredded Cheddar cheese
  Salsa (optional)

In medium nonstick skillet, cook and stir onion and garlic over
medium heat 5 minutes until soft and translucent. Add cooked pork;
toss lightly. Heat thoroughly; stir in jalapeño pepper. On each tortilla,
spoon ¼ cup pork mixture, a portion of lettuce, tomatoes and
1 tablespoon cheese; top with salsa, if desired. *Makes 6 servings*

Prep Time: 15 minutes

Favorite recipe from National Pork Board

Corn & Zucchini Medley

¾ **pound ground beef**
1½ **cups fresh or frozen corn kernels**
2 **small zucchini, chopped**
1 **large tomato, chopped**
½ **cup chopped onion**
1½ **tablespoons chopped fresh thyme** *or* 1½ **teaspoon dried thyme**
1 **tablespoon chopped fresh basil** *or* 1 **teaspoon dried basil**

Brown beef in large skillet over medium-high heat. Drain. Stir in corn, zucchini, tomato, onion, thyme and basil. Cover; cook 10 minutes on medium-low heat or until zucchini is tender. Season to taste with salt and pepper. *Makes 4 servings*

Oriental Stir-Fry

1 **bag SUCCESS® Rice**
  Spicy Oriental Sauce (recipe follows)
¼ **cup safflower oil, divided**
¾ **pound skinless, boneless turkey, cut into strips**
½ **teaspoon minced fresh ginger**
1 **clove garlic, minced**
1 **cup broccoli florets**
1 **medium onion, cut into wedges**
1 **yellow bell pepper, seeded and cut into strips**
2 **medium tomatoes, each cut into 6 wedges**

Prepare rice according to package directions. Prepare Spicy Oriental Sauce; set aside.

Heat 2 tablespoons oil in large skillet or wok. Stir-fry turkey, ginger and garlic until turkey is no longer pink. Remove turkey; set aside.

Heat remaining 2 tablespoons oil in same skillet. Stir-fry broccoli, onion and bell pepper 1 minute. Add turkey and tomatoes. Stir sauce; add to skillet. Cook and stir until sauce is thickened. Serve over hot rice. Garnish, if desired. *Makes 4 servings*

Spicy Oriental Sauce: Combine 2 tablespoons cornstarch, ½ cup water, 2 tablespoons reduced-sodium soy sauce, 1 tablespoon sherry, 1 tablespoon Worcestershire sauce and 1 teaspoon curry powder in small bowl; mix well.

Grilled Pork Tenderloin with Tomato-Mango Salsa

2 pork tenderloins (about ¾ pound each)
⅓ cup reduced-sodium teriyaki sauce
2 medium tomatoes, seeded and diced
1 cup diced mango
½ cup minced yellow or green bell pepper
¼ cup hot jalapeño jelly, melted
2 tablespoons white wine vinegar

1. Prepare grill for direct grilling. Rub pork tenderloins all over with teriyaki sauce; let stand 5 minutes.

2. Combine tomatoes, mango, bell pepper, jelly and vinegar in medium bowl; mix well. Set aside.

3. Grill pork, covered, over medium-hot coals 20 to 25 minutes or until meat thermometer inserted into thickest part registers 160°F, turning once. Slice and serve with salsa. *Makes 6 servings*

Prep and Cook Time: 30 minutes

Deluxe Turkey Pita Melt

1 whole wheat pita bread
2 ounces Brie or other soft cheese, at room temperature
2 ounces sliced smoked turkey
1 medium tomato, thinly sliced
¼ teaspoon dried basil
Alfalfa sprouts or shredded lettuce

1. Preheat oven to 400°F. Cut pita around edge to make 2 flat pieces.

2. Spread inside of each pita half with Brie. Top with turkey, tomato and basil.

3. Place pita halves on baking sheet. Bake about 5 minutes or until cheese melts and topping is hot. Serve warm topped with alfalfa sprouts. *Makes 2 servings*

Grilled Pork Tenderloin with Tomato-Mango Salsa

Border Scramble

1 pound BOB EVANS® Original Recipe Roll Sausage
1½ cups chopped cooked potatoes
1½ cups chopped onions
1½ cups chopped tomatoes
¾ cup chopped green bell pepper
¼ to ½ cup picante sauce
½ to 1 tablespoon hot pepper sauce
½ teaspoon garlic powder
½ teaspoon salt
4 (9-inch) flour tortillas
2 cups prepared meatless chili
½ cup (2 ounces) shredded Cheddar cheese

Crumble sausage into large skillet. Cook over medium heat until browned, stirring occasionally. Drain off any drippings. Add all remaining ingredients except tortillas, chili and cheese; simmer 20 minutes or until vegetables are crisp-tender. To warm tortillas, microwave 1 minute at HIGH between paper towels. Place 1 cup sausage mixture in center of each tortilla; fold tortilla over filling to close. Heat chili in small saucepan until hot, stirring occasionally. Top each folded tortilla with ½ cup chili and 2 tablespoons cheese. Serve hot. Refrigerate leftovers.   *Makes 4 servings*

Tarragon Scallops & Zucchini

1¼ pounds sea scallops
6 tablespoons butter
2 small zucchini, thinly sliced
¼ teaspoon onion powder
2 cups uncooked instant white rice
3 green onions, chopped
3 tablespoons chopped fresh tarragon *or* **¾ teaspoon dried tarragon**
¼ teaspoon salt
2 tablespoons lemon juice
2 teaspoons cornstarch

1. Rinse scallops; pat dry with paper towels. Cut large scallops in half.

2. Melt butter in large nonstick skillet over medium heat. Stir in scallops, zucchini and onion powder; cook and stir 2 minutes. Cover; reduce heat. Cook 7 minutes.

3. Meanwhile, prepare rice according to package directions. Combine green onions, tarragon and salt in small bowl. Blend lemon juice and cornstarch in another small bowl until smooth; set aside.

4. Stir green onion and cornstarch mixtures into skillet. Increase heat to medium; cook and stir 1 minute or until sauce thickens and scallops are opaque. Serve over rice.   *Makes 4 servings*

Serving Suggestions: Steamed carrots and flaky croissant dinner rolls.

Prep and Cook Time: 20 minutes

Easy Pepper Steak

1 pound lean ground beef
1 tablespoon chopped fresh thyme *or* 1 teaspoon dried thyme
1 teaspoon paprika
   Salt and black pepper
3 tablespoons all-purpose flour
1¼ cups chicken broth
2 tablespoons dry white wine
1 teaspoon Worcestershire sauce
1 *each* red, green and yellow medium bell peppers, cut into thin
   slices
1 medium onion, sliced, separated into rings

Microwave Directions
Crumble ground beef into large bowl. Stir in thyme, paprika, 1 teaspoon salt and dash of black pepper. Shape into four ½-inch-thick oval loaves. Place on microwavable rack; cover with waxed paper. Microwave on HIGH 4 to 5 minutes or until cooked through (160°F), turning rack after 3 minutes. Reserve ⅓ cup meat drippings; keep meat warm. Mix drippings and flour in medium microwavable bowl. Stir in broth, wine and Worcestershire sauce. Microwave on HIGH 2 to 3 minutes or until mixture thickens, stirring every minute. Season to taste with salt and black pepper. Add bell peppers and onion; cover. Microwave on HIGH 6 to 7 minutes or until vegetables are crisp-tender, stirring after 3 minutes. Serve over meat. *Makes 4 servings*

PERFECT
PASTA

Tuna Tomato Casserole

2 cans (6 ounces each) tuna, drained
1 cup mayonnaise
1 small onion, finely chopped
¼ teaspoon salt
¼ teaspoon black pepper
1 package (12 ounces) uncooked wide egg noodles
8 to 10 plum tomatoes, sliced ¼ inch thick
1 cup (4 ounces) shredded Cheddar or mozzarella cheese

1. Preheat oven to 375°F.

2. Combine tuna, mayonnaise, onion, salt and pepper in medium bowl; mix well. Set aside.

3. Prepare noodles according to package directions, cooking just until tender. Drain noodles and return to pot.

4. Add tuna mixture to noodles; stir until well blended.

5. Layer half of noodle mixture, half of tomatoes and half of cheese in 13×9-inch baking dish. Press down slightly. Repeat layers with remaining ingredients.

6. Bake 20 minutes or until cheese is melted and casserole is heated through.
Makes 6 servings

Creamy Chicken Primavera

1 teaspoon olive oil
2 medium red, yellow or green bell peppers, coarsely chopped
1 medium onion, chopped
1 pound boneless, skinless chicken breasts, cut into 1-inch pieces
½ cup frozen green peas, thawed
1 jar (16 ounces) RAGÚ® Cheesy!® Light Parmesan Alfredo Sauce
⅛ teaspoon ground black pepper
8 ounces linguine or spaghetti, cooked and drained

1. In 12-inch nonstick skillet, heat olive oil over medium-high heat and cook red bell peppers and onion, stirring occasionally, 10 minutes or until golden.

2. Stir in chicken and peas and continue cooking, stirring occasionally, 5 minutes. Stir in Ragú Cheesy! Sauce and black pepper.

3. Reduce heat to medium and simmer, stirring occasionally, 10 minutes or until chicken is thoroughly cooked. Serve over hot linguine.   *Makes 4 servings*

Confetti Capellini

Non-stick cooking spray
2 cups frozen whole kernel corn, thawed
1 red bell pepper, chopped
1 yellow bell pepper, chopped
¾ cup chopped red onion
1½ cups heavy cream
1 to 2 tablespoons chili powder
2 cups (12 ounces) chopped CURE 81® ham
¼ teaspoon black pepper
12 ounces capellini or angel hair pasta, cooked and drained
2 tomatoes, peeled, seeded and chopped
¼ cup minced fresh cilantro

In skillet coated with cooking spray, sauté corn, bell peppers and onion over medium heat 5 minutes or until tender. Add cream and chili powder. Bring to a boil; boil 5 minutes or until cream has slightly thickened, stirring occasionally. Stir in ham and black pepper. Pour over capellini and toss well. To serve, sprinkle with chopped tomatoes and cilantro.   *Makes 6 servings*

Creamy Chicken Primavera

Bowtie Pasta with Garlic & Grilled Chicken

1¼ pounds boneless skinless chicken breasts
1 package (16 ounces) bowtie pasta
5 tablespoons olive oil
4 cloves garlic, minced
24 ounces shiitake mushrooms, sliced
2 cups chopped seeded plum tomatoes
1 cup chopped green onions
1 teaspoon red pepper flakes
2 cups chicken broth
¼ cup cilantro leaves, chopped, divided

1. Prepare grill for direct grilling.

2. Grill chicken, on covered grill, 6 to 8 minutes or until chicken is no longer pink in center, turning halfway through cooking. Refrigerate chicken until cool enough to handle. Cut chicken into ½-inch cubes; set aside.

3. Cook pasta according to package directions; drain.

4. Meanwhile, heat oil in large skillet over medium heat. Cook and stir garlic 1 minute. Add mushrooms, tomatoes, green onions and red pepper flakes. Cook and stir 2 minutes.

5. Add broth; simmer mixture to reduce slightly. Add chicken, pasta and half of cilantro; heat through. Garnish with remaining cilantro.

Makes 6 to 8 servings

Fire-Roasted Tomatoes with Gemelli Pasta

   4 pounds Roma tomatoes
12 ounces uncooked gemelli, penne or fusilli pasta
   1 shallot, sliced
   ½ to 1 jalapeño pepper,* seeded and coarsely chopped
   1 clove garlic, sliced
20 large fresh basil leaves
   1 tablespoon olive oil
   ¾ teaspoon salt
   ⅛ teaspoon black pepper
   2 ounces reduced-fat goat cheese *or* ¼ cup reduced-fat ricotta cheese

*Jalapeño peppers can sting and irritate the skin. Wear rubber gloves when handling peppers and do not touch your eyes. Wash your hands after handling peppers.

1. Prepare grill for direct grilling.

2. Cut tomatoes in half crosswise; remove seeds. Grill tomatoes, skin sides down, over hot coals about 5 minutes or until skins are blackened and tomatoes are very tender. Place tomatoes in paper bag for 10 minutes; remove skins. Set tomatoes aside.

3. Meanwhile, cook pasta according to package directions, omitting salt. Drain; set aside.

4. Combine shallot, jalapeño pepper and garlic in food processor; process until finely chopped. Add tomatoes, basil, oil, salt and black pepper; process until well blended. Return pasta to pan; pour sauce over pasta. Cook 1 minute, stirring frequently.

5. Remove from heat; stir in cheese. Serve immediately.

Makes 4 (1½-cup) servings

Note: Tomatoes can be broiled rather than grilled. Preheat broiler; seed tomatoes as directed in step 2. Place tomatoes, cut sides down, on broiler pan. Broil tomatoes 5 minutes or until skins are blackened and tomatoes are very tender. Remove skins as directed in step 2.

Fire-Roasted Tomatoes with Gemelli Pasta

Rotini with Summer Vegetables

12 ounces uncooked rotini pasta
 3 cups broccoli florets
 3 cups sliced carrots
 3 medium red bell peppers, cut into 1-inch squares
 ¼ cup water
 ¼ teaspoon plus ⅛ teaspoon red pepper flakes, divided
 3 cups sliced mushrooms
 3 tablespoons olive oil
 3 cloves garlic, minced
 4 cups coarsely chopped seeded peeled plum tomatoes
 ⅓ cup chopped fresh basil leaves
 ¼ cup Chardonnay or other dry white wine
 2 cups (8 ounces) shredded part-skim mozzarella cheese
 ¼ cup shredded Asiago cheese

1. Cook pasta according to package directions; drain. Place in large bowl.

2. Meanwhile, combine broccoli, carrots, bell peppers, water and ¼ teaspoon red pepper flakes in large microwavable baking dish. Cover loosely and microwave on HIGH 5 minutes or until hot. Stir in mushrooms. Cover and microwave 3 minutes. Let stand, covered, 5 minutes.

3. Meanwhile, to prepare sauce, heat oil in medium saucepan over medium-low heat until hot. Add garlic and remaining ⅛ teaspoon red pepper flakes. Cook and stir 1 minute. Add tomatoes. Cook 5 minutes. Stir in basil and wine. Simmer 5 minutes.

4. While sauce is simmering, add vegetables to pasta; toss until blended. Place pasta mixture into serving bowl; sprinkle with cheeses. Serve with sauce.   *Makes 10 servings*

Rotini with Summer Vegetables

Caponata-Style Fettuccine

1 medium eggplant (about 16 ounces), cut into ¼-inch slices
1¼ teaspoons salt, divided
⅓ cup olive oil, divided
1 small green bell pepper, sliced
1 medium onion, coarsely chopped
2 cloves garlic, minced
3 medium tomatoes (about 16 ounces), seeded and coarsely chopped
⅓ cup raisins
⅓ cup halved pitted green olives
¼ cup balsamic or red wine vinegar
2 tablespoons capers, rinsed and drained (optional)
¼ teaspoon *each* ground cinnamon and black pepper
10 ounces fresh spinach fettuccine, cooked, drained and kept warm
Fresh basil leaves

1. Place oven rack at lowest position. Preheat oven to 450°F. Place eggplant slices in large colander over bowl; sprinkle with 1 teaspoon salt. Drain 1 hour.

2. Place eggplant slices in single layer on baking sheet or jelly-roll pan; brush both sides lightly with some of oil. Bake 10 minutes or until lightly browned. Turn slices over; bake about 5 minutes more or until tops are lightly browned and slices are softened; set aside.

3. Heat remaining oil in large skillet over medium-high heat. Add bell pepper; cook and stir 5 minutes or until pepper turns bright green. Remove pepper; set aside.

4. Add onion and garlic to same skillet; cook and stir 5 minutes or until onion is soft. Add tomatoes, raisins, olives, vinegar, capers, if desired, remaining ¼ teaspoon salt, cinnamon and black pepper. Cook until most of the liquid has evaporated.

5. Cut roasted eggplant slices into quarters; add to tomato mixture. Add bell pepper; cook until heated through. Serve over fettuccine. Garnish.

Makes 4 main-dish servings

Note: Caponata is a Sicilian eggplant dish that can be served cold as an appetizer or on lettuce as a salad. Here it is made into a vegetarian sauce for pasta.

Italian Tomato Bake

1 pound sweet Italian sausage, cut into ½-inch slices
2 tablespoons margarine or butter
1 cup chopped onion
4 cups cooked egg noodles
2 cups frozen broccoli florets, thawed and drained
2 cups prepared pasta sauce
½ cup diced plum tomatoes
2 cloves garlic, minced
3 plum tomatoes, sliced
1 cup (8 ounces) low-fat ricotta cheese
⅓ cup grated Parmesan cheese
1 teaspoon dried oregano

1. Preheat oven to 350°F. Cook sausage in large skillet over medium heat about 10 minutes or until barely pink in center. Drain on paper towels; set aside. Drain fat from skillet.

2. Add margarine and onion to skillet; cook and stir until onion is tender. Combine onion, noodles, broccoli, pasta sauce, diced tomatoes and garlic in large bowl; mix well. Transfer to 13×9-inch baking dish.

3. Top with sausage and arrange tomato slices over top. Place 1 heaping tablespoonful ricotta cheese on each tomato slice. Sprinkle casserole with Parmesan cheese and oregano. Bake 35 minutes or until hot and bubbly.   *Makes 6 servings*

Ravioli with Homemade Tomato Sauce

3 cloves garlic
½ cup fresh basil leaves
3 cups seeded peeled tomatoes, cut into quarters
2 tablespoons tomato paste
2 tablespoons fat-free Italian salad dressing
1 tablespoon balsamic vinegar
¼ teaspoon black pepper
1 package (9 ounces) uncooked refrigerated reduced-fat cheese ravioli
2 cups shredded washed spinach leaves
1 cup (4 ounces) shredded part-skim mozzarella cheese

Microwave Directions

1. To prepare tomato sauce, process garlic in food processor until coarsely chopped. Add basil; process until coarsely chopped. Add tomatoes, tomato paste, salad dressing, vinegar and pepper; process, using on/off pulsing action, until tomatoes are chopped.

2. Spray 9-inch square microwavable dish with nonstick cooking spray. Spread 1 cup tomato sauce in dish. Layer half of ravioli and spinach over tomato sauce. Repeat layers with 1 cup tomato sauce and remaining ravioli and spinach. Top with remaining 1 cup tomato sauce. Cover with plastic wrap; refrigerate 1 to 8 hours.

3. Vent plastic wrap. Microwave on MEDIUM (50%) 18 to 20 minutes or until pasta is tender and hot. Sprinkle with cheese. Microwave on HIGH 3 minutes or just until cheese melts. Let stand, covered, 5 minutes before serving.   *Makes 6 servings*

Summer Garden Harvest Fusilli

¼ cup olive oil
8 ounces mushrooms, sliced
1 red bell pepper, diced
1 green bell pepper, diced
1 yellow bell pepper, diced
1 large onion, chopped
10 green onions, chopped
3 shallots, chopped
8 cloves garlic, minced
¼ teaspoon red pepper flakes
4 cups chopped seeded tomatoes
½ cup chopped fresh basil leaves
2 tablespoons chopped fresh oregano
   Salt and black pepper
1 package (16 ounces) fusilli, cooked according to package directions
   and drained

1. Heat oil in large skillet over medium-high heat. Cook and stir mushrooms, bell peppers, onions, shallots, garlic and red pepper flakes until lightly browned. Add tomatoes; bring to a boil. Reduce heat to low; simmer, uncovered, 20 minutes. Stir in basil and oregano. Season to taste with salt and black pepper.

2. Place fusilli on plates. Spoon sauce over fusilli.
                                        Makes 6 to 8 servings

TEMPTING
SIDES

Grilled Vegetables & Brown Rice

1 medium zucchini
1 medium red or yellow bell pepper, quartered lengthwise
1 small onion, cut crosswise into 1-inch-thick slices
¾ cup Italian dressing
4 cups hot cooked UNCLE BEN'S® Original Brown Rice

1. Cut zucchini lengthwise into thirds. Place all vegetables in large resealable plastic food storage bag; add dressing. Seal bag; refrigerate several hours or overnight.

2. Remove vegetables from marinade, reserving marinade. Place bell pepper and onion on grill over medium coals; brush with marinade. Grill 5 minutes. Turn vegetables over; add zucchini. Brush with marinade. Continue grilling until vegetables are crisp-tender, about 5 minutes, turning zucchini over after 3 minutes.

3. Remove vegetables from grill; coarsely chop. Add to hot rice; mix lightly. Season with salt and black pepper, if desired.

Makes 6 to 8 servings

Tip: Grilling adds a unique smokey flavor to vegetables and brings out their natural sweetness. The easiest way to grill vegetables is to cut them into large pieces and toss them in salad dressing or seasoned oil before grilling. Seasoned raw vegetables may also be wrapped tightly in foil packets and grilled until tender.

Stovetop Summer Squash

   3 tablespoons butter
   1 cup chopped onion
   1 cup chopped red bell pepper
   2 cups sliced yellow summer squash
   2 cups sliced zucchini
   1 teaspoon minced fresh basil leaves
1⅔ cups water
   1 package (6 ounces) stuffing mix with herb seasoning packet

1. Melt butter in large skillet over medium heat. Add onion and bell pepper; cook and stir 3 minutes. Add squash, zucchini and basil; cook and stir about 3 minutes or until vegetables are tender.

2. Bring water to a boil in 2-quart saucepan. Add squash mixture, stuffing mix and seasoning packet; mix until all liquid is absorbed. Cover; let stand 5 minutes. Fluff with fork before serving. *Makes 6 servings*

Skillet Corn & Tomatoes

   4 ears fresh corn (or 3 cups frozen)
   3 tablespoons CRISCO® Corn Oil*
   2 cloves garlic, minced
   1 jalapeño pepper, seeded and finely diced
   2 tomatoes, puréed in a blender or food processor
   2 tablespoons butter
   Salt and pepper
¼ cup chopped fresh chives

Or use your favorite Crisco Oil.

Cut corn kernels off the cob with a sharp knife; set aside. Heat CRISCO Oil in a skillet over medium heat; add garlic and jalapeño pepper. Sauté for 2 minutes or until garlic is fragrant but not brown. Add corn and sauté, stirring often, about 3 minutes. Add puréed tomatoes; simmer about 2 minutes. Stir in butter and season to taste with salt and pepper. Add chives. Serve immediately. *Makes 4 to 6 servings*

Prep Time: 10 minutes
Cook Time: 7 minutes

Mediterranean Vegetable Bake

2 tomatoes, sliced
1 small red onion, sliced
1 medium zucchini, sliced
1 small eggplant, sliced
1 large portobello mushroom, sliced
2 cloves garlic, finely chopped
3 tablespoons olive oil
2 teaspoons chopped fresh rosemary
⅔ cup dry white wine
  Salt
  Black pepper

1. Preheat oven to 350°F. Oil bottom of oval casserole or 13×9-inch baking dish.

2. Arrange slices of vegetables in rows, alternating different types and overlapping slices in pan to make attractive arrangement. Sprinkle garlic evenly over top. Mix olive oil with rosemary in small bowl; spread over top.

3. Pour wine over vegetables; season with salt and pepper. Loosely cover with foil. Bake 20 minutes. Uncover and bake an additional 10 to 15 minutes or until vegetables are tender.   *Makes 4 to 6 servings*

Fried Green Tomatoes

  2 medium green tomatoes
  ¼ cup all-purpose flour
  ¼ cup yellow cornmeal
  ½ teaspoon salt
  ½ teaspoon garlic salt
  ½ teaspoon ground red pepper
  ½ teaspoon cracked black pepper
  1 cup buttermilk
  1 cup vegetable oil
    Hot pepper sauce (optional)

1. Cut tomatoes into ¼-inch-thick slices. Combine flour, cornmeal, salt, garlic salt, red pepper and black pepper in pie plate or shallow bowl; mix well. Pour buttermilk into second pie plate or shallow bowl.

2. Heat oil in large skillet over medium heat. Meanwhile, dip tomato slices into buttermilk, coating both sides. Immediately dredge slices in flour mixture; shake off excess flour mixture.

3. Cook tomato slices in hot oil 3 to 5 minutes per side. Transfer to parchment paper or paper towels. Serve immediately with pepper sauce, if desired.   *Makes 3 to 4 servings*

Serving Suggestion: Serve fried green tomatoes with shredded lettuce.

Vegetable Stew Medley

2 tablespoons CRISCO® Oil*
4 medium onions, thinly sliced and separated into rings
3 medium green bell peppers, cut into strips
2 cloves garlic, minced
4 medium zucchini, cut into ½-inch pieces
1 medium eggplant, cut into ½-inch pieces (about 16 ounces)
1 can (14½ ounces) no-salt-added whole tomatoes, drained and
    chopped, *or* 4 or 5 fresh tomatoes, peeled and quartered
1 teaspoon dried dill weed
¾ teaspoon dried basil leaves
½ teaspoon dried oregano leaves
½ teaspoon black pepper
¼ teaspoon salt
1 package (9 ounces) frozen peas
¼ cup lemon juice
2 tablespoons chopped fresh parsley *or* 2 teaspoons dried parsley

Use your favorite Crisco Oil.

1. Heat oil in Dutch oven (non-reactive or non-cast iron) on medium heat. Add onions, bell peppers and garlic. Cook and stir until tender.

2. Add zucchini and eggplant. Cook 5 minutes, stirring occasionally. Stir in tomatoes, dill weed, basil, oregano, black pepper and salt. Reduce heat to low. Cover. Simmer 20 minutes, stirring occasionally.

3. Stir in peas. Simmer 3 to 5 minutes or until peas are thawed and heated, stirring occasionally. Stir in lemon juice. Serve hot or chilled, sprinkled with parsley. *Makes 12 servings*

Vegetable Stew Medley

Festive Corn Casserole

2 cups grated zucchini
1 cup fresh or frozen corn kernels
1 cup diced red bell pepper
2 cups egg substitute
½ cup fat-free evaporated milk
2 teaspoons sugar substitute (optional)
¼ teaspoon celery seeds
⅛ teaspoon salt
⅛ teaspoon red pepper flakes (optional)

1. Preheat oven to 350°F. Coat 11×7×2-inch baking dish with nonstick cooking spray.

2. Mix zucchini, corn and bell pepper in baking dish. Whisk egg substitute, evaporated milk, sugar substitute, if desired, celery seeds, salt and pepper flakes, if desired, together in medium bowl; pour over vegetables in baking dish. Bake 45 to 55 minutes or until set and lightly browned.

Makes 10 servings

Plum Ratatouille

2½ cups diced eggplant
2 cups sliced zucchini
1 onion, cut into wedges
1 tablespoon vegetable oil
2 cups diced tomatoes
2 cups fresh California plum wedges
2 teaspoons minced garlic
1½ teaspoons dried basil leaves, crushed
1 teaspoon dried oregano leaves, crushed
¼ teaspoon pepper
Fresh lemon juice

In large nonstick skillet, cook and stir eggplant, zucchini and onion in oil 15 minutes or until tender. Add remaining ingredients except lemon juice; reduce heat and cover. Cook, stirring occasionally, until plums are tender, about 4 minutes. Drizzle with fresh lemon juice just before serving.

Makes 6 servings

Festive Corn Casserole

Parmesan Vegetable Bake

½ cup seasoned dry bread crumbs
½ cup grated Parmesan cheese
2 tablespoons butter, cut into small pieces
1 clove garlic, minced
1 teaspoon dried oregano
¼ teaspoon black pepper
1 large baking potato, cut into ¼-inch-thick slices
1 medium zucchini, cut diagonally into ¼-inch-thick slices
1 large tomato, cut into ¼-inch-thick slices

1. Preheat oven to 375°F. Spray shallow 1-quart casserole with nonstick cooking spray.

2. Combine bread crumbs, Parmesan cheese, butter, garlic, oregano and pepper in small bowl; mix well. Arrange potato slices in prepared casserole, overlapping slightly. Sprinkle with ⅓ crumb mixture. Top with zucchini slices; sprinkle with ⅓ crumb mixture. Top with tomato slices. Sprinkle with remaining crumb mixture.

3. Cover; bake 40 minutes. Remove cover; bake 10 minutes more or until vegetables are tender.   *Makes 4 servings*

Tip: Tomatoes should never be refrigerated before cutting, because cold temperatures cause their flesh to become mealy and lose flavor. Instead, store them at room temperature out of direct sunlight.

Beefsteak Tomatoes with Chunky Blue Cheese Vinaigrette

¼ **cup white wine vinegar**
1 **tablespoon Dijon mustard**
¼ **teaspoon salt**
⅛ **teaspoon pepper**
  Pinch of sugar
¾ **cup CRISCO® Canola Oil***
¾ **cup crumbled blue cheese**
4 **large, ripe beefsteak tomatoes, core removed, cut into thick slices**
  Fresh basil sprigs for garnish
  Additional salt and pepper

*Or use your favorite Crisco Oil.

In a small plastic container with tight-fitting lid, combine the vinegar, Dijon mustard, salt, pepper and sugar; shake well. Pour in CRISCO Oil and shake until well blended. Add crumbled blue cheese; shake to mix. Pour over tomato slices; garnish with fresh basil. Season to taste with salt and pepper. Refrigerate any unused dressing.

Makes 4 to 6 servings

Prep Time: 10 minutes

SALADS &
SANDWICHES

Zesty Zucchini & Chick-Pea Salad

3 medium zucchini (about 6 ounces each)
½ teaspoon salt
5 tablespoons white vinegar
1 clove garlic, minced
¼ teaspoon dried thyme
½ cup olive oil
1 cup drained canned chick-peas
½ cup sliced pitted ripe olives
3 green onions, minced
1 ripe avocado, cut into ½-inch cubes
⅓ cup crumbled feta cheese *or* 3 tablespoons grated Romano cheese
1 canned chipotle pepper in adobo sauce, drained, seeded and minced
1 head Boston lettuce, separated into leaves
Sliced tomatoes and cilantro sprigs (optional)

1. Cut zucchini lengthwise into halves; cut halves crosswise into ¼-inch-thick slices. Place slices in medium bowl; sprinkle with salt. Toss to mix. Spread zucchini on several layers of paper towels. Let stand at room temperature 30 minutes to drain.

2. Combine vinegar, garlic and thyme in large bowl. Gradually add oil, whisking continuously until dressing is thoroughly blended.

3. Pat zucchini dry; add to dressing. Add chick-peas, olives and onions; toss lightly to coat. Cover and refrigerate at least 30 minutes or up to 4 hours, stirring occasionally.

4. Add avocado, cheese and pepper to salad just before serving; toss gently to mix.

5. Serve salad on lettuce leaves. Garnish with tomatoes and cilantro.
Makes 4 to 6 servings

Tuscan Vegetable Wrappers

  2 teaspoons olive oil
  1 large onion, thinly sliced
  2 red and/or green bell peppers, thinly sliced
  1 package (10 ounces) sliced mushrooms
1½ cups RAGÚ® Organic Pasta Sauce
  ⅛ teaspoon ground black pepper
  1 package (12 ounces) flour tortillas, warmed
  2 tablespoons grated Parmesan cheese

In 12-inch nonstick skillet, heat olive oil over medium-high heat and cook onion, red peppers and mushrooms, stirring occasionally, 10 minutes or until vegetables are tender. Stir in Pasta Sauce and black pepper.

Bring to a boil over high heat. Reduce heat to low and simmer 5 minutes.

Evenly spoon about ⅓ cup vegetable mixture onto tortillas, sprinkle with cheese, then roll. To serve, arrange seam side down on serving plate and top with remaining vegetable mixture.   *Makes 6 servings*

Prep Time: 10 minutes
Cook Time: 20 minutes

Tuscan Vegetable Wrapper

Sausage, Pepper & Onion Heroes

1 green bell pepper
1 yellow or red bell pepper
2 tablespoons olive oil, divided
4 slices (¼ inch) red or yellow onion, separated into rings
1 package JENNIE-O TURKEY STORE® Sweet Lean Italian Sausage
5 hoagie or submarine sandwich rolls, split, toasted if desired
¾ cup prepared pizza or spaghetti sauce, heated

Prepare grill or preheat broiler. Cut bell peppers lengthwise into ¼-inch strips. Heat 1 tablespoon oil in large skillet over medium heat. Add pepper strips and onion rings; cook about 15 minutes or until vegetables are tender, stirring frequently. Sprinkle lightly with salt, if desired. Meanwhile, brush remaining 1 tablespoon of oil over sausages. Grill or broil about 5 inches from heat source 14 to 16 minutes or until lightly browned and no longer pink in center, turning occasionally. Serve sausages in rolls topped with pizza sauce and vegetables.

Makes 5 servings

Cook Time: 15 minutes

Turkey and Bean Tostadas

6 (8-inch) flour tortillas
1 pound lean ground turkey
1 can (15 ounces) chili beans in chili sauce
½ teaspoon chili powder
3 cups washed and shredded romaine lettuce
1 large tomato, chopped
¼ cup chopped fresh cilantro
¼ cup (1 ounce) shredded reduced-fat Monterey Jack cheese
½ cup reduced-fat sour cream (optional)

1. Preheat oven to 350°F. Place tortillas on baking sheets. Bake 7 minutes or until crisp. Place on individual plates.

2. Meanwhile, brown turkey in large nonstick skillet over medium-high heat. Drain fat. Add beans and chili powder. Cook 5 minutes over medium heat. Divide turkey mixture evenly among tortillas. Top with remaining ingredients and sour cream, if desired. *Makes 6 servings*

Roasted Tomato and Mozzarella Pasta Salad

3 cups (8 ounces) rotelle pasta, uncooked
3 cups Roasted Fresh Tomatoes (recipe follows)
1 cup green bell pepper, cut into ½-inch pieces
¾ cup (3 ounces) cubed mozzarella cheese (½-inch cubes)
¼ cup chopped mild red onion
½ teaspoon salt
¼ teaspoon black pepper
⅓ cup prepared red wine vinaigrette salad dressing

Cook pasta according to package directions; rinse and drain. Place pasta in large bowl. Cut Roasted Fresh Tomatoes into chunks; add to pasta. Add bell pepper, mozzarella, onion, salt and black pepper to pasta. Pour salad dressing over top; toss to combine. Garnish with fresh basil leaves, if desired. *Makes 4 servings*

Roasted Fresh Tomatoes

6 large (about 3 pounds) Florida tomatoes
2 tablespoons vegetable oil
½ teaspoon dried basil leaves
¼ teaspoon dried thyme leaves
¼ teaspoon salt
¼ teaspoon black pepper

Preheat oven to 425°F. Use tomatoes held at room temperature until fully ripe. Core tomatoes; cut into halves horizontally. Gently squeeze halves to remove seeds. Place cut sides up on rack in broiler pan; set aside. Combine oil, basil, thyme, salt and pepper in small bowl; brush over cut sides of tomatoes. Place tomatoes cut sides down on rack. Bake about 30 minutes or until well browned. Remove skins, if desired. Serve hot, warm or cold. *Makes 4 to 6 servings*

Favorite recipe from Florida Tomato Committee

Ranch Tuna Stuffed Tomatoes

1 can (6 ounces) solid white tuna, drained
1 can (8 ounces) kidney beans, rinsed and drained
1 can (8 ounces) corn, drained
1 cup (4 ounces) shredded mild Cheddar cheese
⅔ cup HIDDEN VALLEY® The Original Ranch® Dressing
¼ cup chopped green onions
4 large fresh tomatoes (at least 8 ounces each)

Flake tuna and combine with beans, corn, cheese, dressing and onions in a medium bowl. Cover and chill 1 hour. Just before serving, core each tomato and carefully scoop out center to within ¼ inch of edge forming a bowl; discard flesh and seeds. Drain tomatoes upside down on paper towels. Cut each tomato into 5 or 6 wedges, leaving the bottom intact. Gently open each tomato to support the salad. Arrange tuna mixture on top of the tomatoes.   *Makes 4 servings*

New Wave BLT

¼ cup mayonnaise
2 tablespoons chopped fresh basil leaves
8 slices whole wheat bread, lightly toasted
8 slices crisply cooked bacon
4 slices large ripe tomato
4 slices SARGENTO® Deli Style Sliced Swiss Cheese
4 leaves romaine or red leaf lettuce

Combine mayonnaise and basil; spread evenly over one side of each slice of toast. Layer bacon, tomato, cheese and lettuce on four slices of toast; close with remaining four slices of toast. Cut each sandwich diagonally in half.   *Makes 4 servings*

Prep Time: 20 minutes

Ranch Tuna Stuffed Tomato

Open-Faced Italian Focaccia Sandwich

    2 cups shredded cooked chicken
    ½ cup HIDDEN VALLEY® The Original Ranch® Salad Dressing
    ¼ cup diagonally sliced green onions
    1 piece focaccia bread, about ¾-inch thick, 10×7 inches
    2 medium tomatoes, thinly sliced
    4 cheese slices, such as provolone, Cheddar or Swiss
    2 tablespoons grated Parmesan cheese (optional)

Stir together chicken, dressing and onions in a small mixing bowl. Arrange chicken mixture evenly on top of focaccia. Top with layer of tomatoes and cheese slices. Sprinkle with Parmesan cheese, if desired. Broil 2 minutes or until cheese is melted and bubbly.

Makes 4 servings

Note: Purchase rotisserie chicken at your favorite store to add great taste and save on preparation time.

Roasted Fresh Tomato Salad with Shells and Chicken

    1½ cups small shell pasta, uncooked
    3 cups Roasted Fresh Tomatoes (recipe page 68)
    1 cup (6 ounces) cooked chicken, cut in ½-inch cubes
    1 cup frozen green peas, thawed
    ½ cup crumbled feta cheese
    ½ cup sliced ripe olives
    ¼ cup sliced scallions (green onions)
    ⅓ cup prepared ranch salad dressing

Cook pasta according to package directions; drain and rinse. Place in large bowl. Cut Roasted Fresh Tomatoes into chunks; add tomatoes, chicken, peas, feta cheese, olives and scallions. Pour salad dressing over all; toss to coat. Serve, if desired, on lettuce-lined plates sprinkled with parsley.

Makes 4 to 6 servings

Favorite recipe from Florida Tomato Committee

Open-Faced Italian Focaccia Sandwich

Grilled Vegetable Paninis

½ cup *French's®* *Gourmayo™* Caesar Ranch Light Mayonnaise
1 teaspoon finely minced garlic
2 small zucchini or yellow squash, cut lengthwise into ¼-inch slices
1 small Japanese eggplant, cut lengthwise into ¼-inch slices
1 red bell pepper, cut into ½-inch strips
8 thick slices round sourdough or Italian bread
1 jar (6 ounces) marinated artichoke hearts, drained and chopped
8 slices mozzarella cheese

1. Combine mayonnaise and garlic; set aside. Coat vegetables with olive oil cooking spray.

2. Heat an electric grill pan until hot. Working in batches, grill vegetables in a single layer for 3 to 5 minutes until tender. Set aside.

3. Spread mayonnaise mixture on one side of bread slices. Layer artichokes and vegetables on 4 slices. Top each with 2 slices cheese. Cover with remaining bread, mayonnaise-side down. Grill sandwiches 3 minutes or just until cheese melts. Cut in half to serve.

Makes 4 servings

Prep Time: 15 minutes
Cook Time: 25 minutes

Chicken Caesar

1 package (about 1 pound) PERDUE® Seasoned Boneless Chicken Breast, Lemon Pepper
1 head romaine lettuce, washed and torn into pieces
½ cup prepared Caesar salad dressing, divided
2 ripe tomatoes, cut into wedges
1 cup Caesar-seasoned croutons

Prepare outdoor grill for direct cooking or preheat broiler. Grill or broil chicken 6 to 8 inches from heat source 6 to 8 minutes per side, until cooked through. Toss lettuce with ⅓ cup salad dressing. Slice chicken and serve warm on bed of lettuce; garnish with tomato slices and top with croutons. Before serving, drizzle with additional dressing.

Makes 4 servings

Prep Time: 10 minutes
Cook Time: 15 minutes

Grilled Vegetable Panini

Hidden Valley® Wraps

1 cup HIDDEN VALLEY® The Original Ranch® Salad Dressing
1 package (8 ounces) cream cheese, softened
10 ounces sliced turkey breast
10 ounces Monterey Jack cheese slices
2 large avocados, peeled and thinly sliced
2 medium tomatoes, thinly sliced
    Shredded lettuce
4 (12-inch) flour tortillas, warmed

Beat together dressing and cream cheese. Evenly layer half the turkey, Monterey Jack cheese, dressing mixture, avocados, tomatoes and lettuce among tortillas, leaving a 1-inch border around edges. Repeat layering with remaining ingredients. Fold right and left edges of tortillas into centers over the filling. Fold the bottom edge toward the center and roll firmly until completely wrapped. Place seam side down and cut in half diagonally. *Makes 4 servings*

Grilled Panini Sandwiches

8 slices country Italian, sourdough or other firm-textured bread
8 slices SARGENTO® Deli Style Sliced Mozzarella Cheese
⅓ cup prepared pesto
4 large slices ripe tomato
2 tablespoons olive oil

1. Top each of 4 slices of bread with a slice of cheese. Spread pesto over cheese. Arrange tomatoes on top, then another slice of cheese. Close sandwiches with remaining 4 slices bread.

2. Brush olive oil lightly over both sides of sandwiches. Cook sandwiches over medium-low coals or in a preheated ridged grill pan over medium heat 3 to 4 minutes per side or until bread is toasted and cheese is melted. *Makes 4 servings*

Prep Time: 5 minutes
Cook Time: 8 minutes

THE BEST OF THE REST

Chocolate Zucchini Snack Cake

1⅔ cups sugar
½ cup (1 stick) butter, softened
½ cup vegetable oil
2 eggs
1½ teaspoons vanilla
2½ cups all-purpose flour
⅓ cup unsweetened cocoa powder
1 teaspoon baking soda
½ teaspoon salt
½ cup buttermilk
2 cups shredded zucchini
1 cup semisweet chocolate chips
¾ cup chopped pecans

1. Preheat oven to 325°F. Grease and flour 13×9-inch baking pan.

2. Beat sugar, butter and oil in large bowl with electric mixer at medium speed until well blended.

3. Add eggs, one at a time, beating well after each addition. Blend in vanilla.

4. Combine flour, cocoa, baking soda and salt in medium bowl. Add to butter mixture alternately with buttermilk, beating well after each addition. Stir in zucchini.

5. Pour into prepared pan. Sprinkle with chocolate chips and pecans.

6. Bake 55 minutes or until toothpick inserted into center comes out clean; cool on wire rack. Cut into squares.

Makes one 13×9-inch cake

Roasted Sweet Pepper Tapas

2 red bell peppers (8 ounces each)
2 tablespoons olive oil
1 teaspoon chopped fresh oregano *or* **½ teaspoon dried oregano**
1 clove garlic, minced
Garlic bread (optional)

1. Adjust rack so that broiler pan is about 4 inches from heat source. Preheat broiler. Cover broiler pan with foil. Place peppers on foil. Broil 15 to 20 minutes or until blackened on all sides, turning peppers every 5 minutes with tongs.

2. To loosen skin, place peppers in paper bag. Close bag; let stand 15 to 20 minutes.

3. To peel peppers, remove core; cut peppers in half. Peel off skin with paring knife, rinsing under cold water to remove seeds and loose skin. Cut peppers into ½-inch strips.

4. Transfer pepper strips to glass jar. Add oil, oregano and garlic. Close lid; shake to blend. Marinate at least 1 hour. Serve on plates with garlic bread or refrigerate in jar up to 1 week.

Makes 6 appetizer servings

Tip: Use this roasting technique for all types of sweet and hot peppers. Broiling time will vary depending on size of pepper. When handling hot peppers, such as Anaheim, jalapeño, poblano or serrano, wear plastic disposable gloves and use caution to prevent irritation to skin or eyes. Green bell peppers do not work as well since their skins are thinner.

Zucchini Chow Chow

  2 cups thinly sliced zucchini
  2 cups thinly sliced yellow summer squash*
  ½ cup thinly sliced red onion
    Salt
 1½ cups cider vinegar
  1 to 1¼ cups sugar
1½ tablespoons pickling spice
  1 cup thinly sliced carrots
  1 small red bell pepper, thinly sliced

*If yellow summer squash is not available, increase zucchini to 4 cups.

1. Sprinkle zucchini, summer squash and onion lightly with salt; let stand in colander 30 minutes. Rinse well with cold water; drain thoroughly. Pat dry with paper towels.

2. Combine vinegar, sugar and pickling spice in medium saucepan. Bring to a boil over high heat. Add carrots, bell pepper and zucchini mixture; bring to a boil. Remove from heat; cool to room temperature.

3. Spoon mixture into sterilized jars; cover and refrigerate up to 3 weeks.
Makes about 8 cups

Black Bean & Corn Salsa

  ¼ cup HELLMANN'S® or BEST FOODS® Light Mayonnaise or
    JUST 2 GOOD!® Mayonnaise Dressing
  2 tablespoons lime juice
  ½ teaspoon ground cumin
  1 can (19 ounces) black beans, rinsed and drained
  1 can (11 ounces) whole kernel corn, drained
  1 cup quartered grape tomatoes or cherry tomatoes
  ½ cup chopped red onion
  2 tablespoons chopped fresh cilantro
  1 teaspoon chopped jalapeño pepper (optional)

1. In medium bowl, blend Hellmann's or Best Foods Light Mayonnaise, lime juice and cumin. Stir in remaining ingredients. Serve chilled or at room temperature.
Makes 4 servings

Prep Time: 10 minutes

Classic Salsa

4 medium tomatoes
1 small onion, finely chopped
2 to 3 jalapeño peppers or serrano peppers,* seeded and minced
¼ cup chopped fresh cilantro
2 tablespoons lime juice
1 small clove garlic, minced
Salt and black pepper

*Jalapeño and serrano peppers can sting and irritate the skin. Wear rubber gloves when handling peppers and do not touch your eyes. Wash your hands after handling peppers.

Cut tomatoes in half; remove seeds. Coarsely chop tomatoes. Combine tomatoes, onion, jalapeño peppers, cilantro, lime juice and garlic in medium bowl. Season to taste with salt and black pepper. Cover and refrigerate 1 hour or up to 3 days for flavors to blend.

Makes about 2½ cups

Warm Tomato-Pepper Sauce

2½ quarts chopped red bell peppers
5 cups thinly sliced green onions
3 tablespoons minced garlic
⅓ cup olive oil
8 quarts California tomatoes, seeded and diced
1⅔ cups grated Parmesan cheese
1 cup chopped parsley
2½ teaspoons black pepper
¾ teaspoon cayenne pepper
3 pounds penne pasta, cooked

1. Sauté bell peppers, onions and garlic in oil in large skillet over medium-high heat until vegetables are tender-crisp.

2. Stir in tomatoes; cook over high heat until sauce thickens, 10 to 15 minutes.

3. Stir in remaining ingredients except pasta. Serve sauce over hot pasta.

Makes 24 servings

Favorite recipe from California Tomato Commission

Tangy Orange Red Pepper Relish

4 large red bell peppers, roasted, skinned and coarsely chopped *or*
    1 (15-ounce) jar roasted red peppers, drained
2 tablespoons cider vinegar
1 clove garlic
½ cup SMUCKER'S® Sweet Orange Marmalade
1 tablespoon cornstarch
2 tablespoons cold water
1 teaspoon hot pepper sauce

In food processor or blender, place red peppers, vinegar and garlic; purée into smooth paste. Add marmalade; blend. Pour relish into small saucepan.

Dissolve cornstarch in cold water; stir into relish. Simmer over high heat 5 minutes or until slightly thickened. Remove from heat; stir in hot pepper sauce. Pour relish into serving bowl; cool.

Makes 1½ cups relish

Note: To roast red peppers, cut in half and remove seeds. Place cut-sides-down on broiler pan. Broil for 10 minutes or until skins are charred. When cool, peel skins from peppers.

Note: Serve this relish with grilled hot dogs or with your favorite grilled meats, poultry or fish.

Summer's Gold Medal Salsa

4 fresh ripe California nectarines
1 fresh ripe pear or apple
2 red bell peppers, seeded and chopped
3 tablespoons minced mild or hot fresh chile peppers
3 tablespoons minced onion
3 tablespoons fresh lime juice

Chop nectarines and pear. Mix all ingredients well, stirring to bring out some juices. Cover with plastic wrap; chill until ready to serve. May be made up to 4 hours ahead.

Makes 6 (½-cup) servings

Favorite recipe from California Tree Fruit Agreement

Double Chocolate Zucchini Muffins

2⅓ cups all-purpose flour
1¼ cups sugar
⅓ cup unsweetened cocoa powder
2 teaspoons baking powder
1½ teaspoons ground cinnamon
1 teaspoon baking soda
½ teaspoon salt
1 cup sour cream
½ cup vegetable oil
2 eggs, beaten
¼ cup milk
1 cup milk chocolate chips
1 cup shredded zucchini

1. Preheat oven to 400°F. Grease 12 (3½-inch) jumbo muffin cups.

2. Combine flour, sugar, cocoa, baking powder, cinnamon, baking soda and salt in large bowl. Combine sour cream, oil, eggs and milk in small bowl until blended; stir into flour mixture just until moistened. Fold in chips and zucchini. Spoon into prepared muffin cups, filling half full.

3. Bake 25 to 30 minutes or until toothpick inserted into centers comes out clean. Cool in pan on wire rack 5 minutes. Remove muffins from pan to wire rack; cool completely. Store tightly covered at room temperature. *Makes 12 jumbo muffins*

Roasted Tomato Sauce

20 ripe plum tomatoes (about 2⅔ pounds), cut in half and seeded
3 tablespoons olive oil, divided
½ teaspoon salt
⅓ cup minced fresh basil leaves
½ teaspoon black pepper

Preheat oven to 450°F. Toss tomatoes with 1 tablespoon oil and salt. Place, cut sides down, on nonstick baking sheet. Bake 20 to 25 minutes or until skins are blistered. Place in paper bag for 10 minutes; remove skins. Process tomatoes, remaining 2 tablespoons oil, basil and pepper in food processor until smooth. *Makes about 1 cup*

Zucchini-Orange Bread

1 package (about 17 ounces) cranberry-orange muffin mix
1½ cups shredded zucchini (about 6 ounces)
1 cup water
1 teaspoon ground cinnamon
1 teaspoon grated orange peel (optional)
Cream cheese (optional)

1. Preheat oven 350°F. Grease 8×4×3-inch loaf pan; set aside.

2. Combine muffin mix, zucchini, water, cinnamon and orange peel, if desired, in medium bowl; stir just until moistened. Spoon batter into prepared loaf pan; bake 40 minutes or until toothpick inserted into center comes out almost clean.

3. Cool in pan on wire rack 15 minutes. Remove bread from pan to wire rack; cool completely. Serve plain or with cream cheese, if desired.

Makes about 16 slices

Tom's Basic Tomato Sauce

3 pounds fresh plum tomatoes, seeded and chopped
½ cup diced onion
½ cup red wine
4 cloves garlic, minced
1 tablespoon sugar (optional)
1 tablespoon dried parsley
1 teaspoon dried basil
¼ teaspoon salt
¼ teaspoon black pepper

1. Place tomatoes in large covered saucepan; cook over medium heat 30 minutes, stirring occasionally.

2. Add onion, wine, garlic, sugar, if desired, parsley, basil, salt and pepper.

3. Simmer sauce slowly, with cover ajar slightly, 3 to 4 hours.

Makes 4 cups sauce

Salsa Cruda

1 cup chopped tomato
2 tablespoons minced onion
2 tablespoons minced fresh cilantro
2 tablespoons lime juice
½ jalapeño pepper,* seeded and minced
3 cloves garlic, minced

Jalapeño peppers can sting and irritate the skin. Wear rubber gloves when handling peppers and do not touch your eyes. Wash your hands after handling peppers.

Combine all ingredients in small bowl; mix well. Serve with tortilla chips.
Makes 4 servings

Honey Strawberry Salsa

1½ cups diced red bell peppers
1 cup sliced fresh strawberries
1 cup diced green bell pepper
1 cup diced fresh tomato
¼ cup chopped Anaheim pepper
2 tablespoons finely chopped fresh cilantro
⅓ cup honey
¼ cup lemon juice
1 tablespoon tequila (optional)
½ teaspoon crushed dried red chili pepper
½ teaspoon salt
¼ teaspoon pepper

Combine ingredients in glass container; mix well. Cover tightly and refrigerate overnight to allow flavors to blend. Serve on grilled fish or chicken.
Makes 3 to 4 cups

Favorite recipe from National Honey Board

Acknowledgments
❧ 91 ❧

The publisher would like to thank the companies and organizations listed below for the use of their recipes and photographs in this publication.

Alouette® Cheese, Chavrie® Cheese, Saladena®

Bays English Muffin Corporation

BelGioioso® Cheese, Inc.

Bob Evans®

Cabot® Creamery Cooperative

California Tomato Commission

California Tree Fruit Agreement

Crisco is a registered trademark of The J.M. Smucker Company

Florida Tomato Committee

The Hidden Valley® Food Products Company

Hormel Foods, LLC

Jennie-O Turkey Store®

MASTERFOODS USA

National Honey Board

National Pork Board

Perdue Farms Incorporated

Reckitt Benckiser Inc.

Riviana Foods Inc.

Sargento® Foods Inc.

Smucker's® trademark of The J.M. Smucker Company

Unilever Foods North America

INDEX
92

INDEX
94